Edmund Spenser - The Shepheardes Calender

Edmund Spenser was born in 1552 in East Smithfield, London.

He was schooled at Merchant Taylors' School and Pembroke College, Cambridge.

Published below is The Shepheardes Clendar is a much admired work that was first published in 1579.

In July of 1580, he departed for Ireland in the service of the newly appointed Lord Deputy, Arthur Grey, 14th Baron Grey de Wilton. Grey was recalled but Spenser stayed, having now acquired official posts and lands in the Munster Plantation.

In 1590, Spenser brought out the first three books of his most famous work, The Faerie Queene. Its success enabled him to obtain a life pension of £50 a year from the Queen.

By 1594, Spenser's first wife had died, and that year he married Elizabeth Boyle, to whom he addressed the sonnet sequence Amoretti. The marriage itself was celebrated in Epithalamion.

In 1596, Spenser wrote a prose pamphlet titled, A View of the Present State of Ireland. This piece, in the form of a dialogue, circulated in manuscript, argued that Ireland would never be totally 'pacified' by the English until its indigenous language and customs had been destroyed, if necessary by violence.

In 1598, during the Nine Years War, Spenser was driven from his home by the native Irish forces of Aodh Ó Néill.

In 1599, Spenser traveled to London, where he died at the age of forty-six. His coffin was carried to his grave in Westminster Abbey by other poets, who threw many pens and pieces of poetry into his grave with many tears.

Index Of Contents

The Shepheardes Calender: Januarie

A Shepeheards boye (no better doe him call)
when Winters wastful spight was almost spent,
All in a sunneshine day, as did befall,
Led forth his flock, that had been long ypent.
So faynt they woxe, and feeble in the folde,
That now vnnethes their feete could them vphold.

All as the Sheepe, such was the shepeheards looke,
For pale and wanne he was, (alas the while,)
May seeme he lovd, or els some care he tooke:
Well couth he tune his pipe, and frame his stile.
Tho to a hill his faynting flocke he ledde,
And thus him playnd, the while his shepe there fedde.

Ye gods of loue, that pitie louers payne,
(if any gods the paine of louers pitie):
Looke from aboue, where you in ioyes remaine,
And bowe your eares vnto my doleful dittie.
And Pan thou shepheards God, that once didst loue,
Pitie the paines, that thou thy selfe didst proue.

Thou barrein ground, whome winters wrath hath wasted,
Art made a myrrhour, to behold my plight:
Whilome thy fresh spring flowrd, and after hasted
Thy sommer prowde with Daffadillies dight.
And now is come thy wynters stormy state,
Thy mantle mard, wherein thou mas-kedst late.

Such rage as winters, reigneth in my heart,
My life bloud friesing wtih vnkindly cold:
Such stormy stoures do breede my balefull smarte,
As if my yeare were wast, and woxen old.
And yet alas, but now my spring begonne,
And yet alas, yt is already donne.

You naked trees, whose shady leaves are lost,
Wherein the byrds were wont to build their bowre:
And now are clothd with mosse and hoary frost,
Instede of bloosmes, wherwith your buds did flowre:
I see your teares, that from your boughes doe raine,
Whose drops in drery ysicles remaine.

All so my lustfull leafe is drye and sere,
My timely buds with wayling all are wasted:
The blossome, which my braunch of youth did beare,
With breathed sighes is blowne away, & blasted,
And from mine eyes the drizling teares descend,
As on your boughes the ysicles depend.

Thou feeble flocke, whose fleece is rough and rent,
Whose knees are weak through fast and evill fare:

Mayst witnesse well by thy ill gouernement,
Thy maysters mind is ouercome with care.
Thou weak, I wanne: thou leabe, I quite forlorne:
With mourning pyne I, you with pyning mourne.

A thousand sithes I curse that carefull hower,
Wherein I longd the neighbour towne to see:
And eke tenne thousand sithes I blesse the stoure,
Wherein I sawe so fayre a sight, as shee.
Yet all for naught: snch [such] sight hath bred my bane.
Ah God, that loue should breede both ioy and payne.

It is not Hobbinol, wherefore I plaine,
Albee my loue he seeke with dayly suit:
His clownish gifts and curtsies I disdaine,
His kiddes, his cracknelles, and his early fruit.
Ah foolish Hobbinol, thy gyfts bene vayne:
Colin them gives to Rosalind againe.

I loue thilke lasse, (alas why doe I loue?)
And am forlorne, (alas why am I lorne?)
Shee deignes not my good will, but doth reproue,
And of my rurall musick holdeth scorne.
Shepheards deuise she hateth as the snake,
And laughes the songes, that Colin Clout doth make.

Wherefore my pype, albee rude Pan thou please,
Yet for thou pleasest not, where most I would:
And thou vnlucky Muse, that wontst to ease
My musing mynd, yet canst not, when thou should:
Both pype and Muse, shall sore the while abye.
So broke his oaten pype, and downe dyd lye.

By that, the welked Phoebus gan availe,
His weary waine, and nowe the frosty Night
Her mantle black through heauen gan overhaile.
Which seene, the pensife boy halfe in despight
Arose, and homeward drove his sonned sheepe,
Whose hanging heads did seeme his carefull case to weepe.

The Shepheardes Calender: Februarie
CVDDIE.
AH for pittie, wil ranke Winters rage,
These bitter blasts neuer ginne tasswage?
The keene cold blowes throug my beaten hyde,
All as I were through the body gryde.
My ragged rontes all shiver and shake,
As doen high Towers in an earthquake:
They wont in the wind wagge their wrigle tailes,
Perke as Peacock: but nowe it auales.

THENOT.
Lewdly complainest thou laesie ladde,
Of Winters wracke, for making thee sadde.
Must not the world wend in his commun course
From good to badd, and from badde to worse,
From worse vnto that is worst of all,
And then returne to his former fall?
Who will not suffer the stormy time,
Where will he liue tyll the lusty prime?
Selfe haue I worne out thrise threttie yeares,
Some in much ioy, many in many teares:
Yet never complained of cold nor heate,
Of Sommers flame, nor of Winters threat:
Ne euer was to Fortune foeman,
But gently tooke, that vngently came.
And euer my flocke was my chiefe care,
Winter or Sommer they mought well fare.

CVDDIE.
No marueile Thenot, if thou can not beare
Cherefully the Winters wrathfull cheare:
For Age and Winter accord full nie,
This chill, that cold, this crooked, that wrye.
And as the lowring Wether lookes downe,
So semest thou like good fryday to frowne.
But my flowring youth is foe to frost,
My shippe vnwont in stormes to be tost.

THENOT.
The soueraigne of seas he blames in vaine,
That once seabeate, will to sea againe.
So loytring liue you little heardgroomes,
Keeping your beastes in the budded broomes:
And when the shining sunne laugheth once,
You deemen, the Spring is come attonce.
Tho gynne you, fond flyes, the cold to scorn,
And crowing in pypes made of greene corne,
You thinken to be Lords of the yeare.
But eft, when ye count you freed from feare,
Comes the breme winter with chamfred browes,
Full of wrinckles and frostie furrowes:
Drerily shooting his stormy darte,
Which cruddles the blood, and pricks the harte.
Then is your carelesse corage accoied,
Your carefull heards with cold bene annoied.
Then paye you the price of your surqedrie,
With weeping, and wayling, and misery.

CVDDIE.
Ah foolish old man, I scorne thy skill,
That wouldest me, my springing yougth to spil.
I deeme, thy braine emperished bee

Through rusty elde, that hath rotted thee:
Or sicker thy head veray tottie is,
So on thy corbe shoulder it leanes amisse.
Now thy selfe hast lost both lopp and topp,
Als my budding branch thou wouldest cropp:
But were thy yeares greene, as now bene myne,
To other delights they would encline.
Tho wouldest thou learne to caroll of Loue,
And hery with hymnes thy lasses gloue.
Tho wouldest thou pype of Phyllis prayse:
But Phyllis is myne for many dayes:
I wonne her with a girdle of gelt,
Embost with buegle about the belt.
Such an one shepeheards woulde make full faine:
Such an one would make thee younge againe.

THENOT.
Thou art a fon, of thy loue to boste,
All that is lent to loue, wyll be lost.

CVDDIE.
Seest, howe brag yond Bullocke beares,
So smirke, so smoothe, his pricked eares?
His hornes bene as broade, as Rainebowe bent,
His dewelap as lythe, as lasse of Kent.
See howe he venteth into the wynd.
Weenest of loue is not his mynd?
Seemeth thy flock thy counsell can,
So lustlesse bene they, so weake so wan,
Clothed with cold, and hoary wyth frost.
Thy flocks father his corage hath lost:
Thy Ewes, that wont to haue blowen bags,
Like wailful widdowes hangen their crags:
The rather Lambes bene starued with cold,
All for their Maister is lustlesse and old.

THENOT.
Cuddie, I wote thou kenst little good,
So vainely taduance thy headlesse hood.
For Youngth is a bubble blown vp with breath,
Whose witt is weakenesse, whose wage is death,
Whose way is wildernesse, whose ynne Penaunce,
And stoopegallaunt Age the hoste of Greeuance.
But shall I tel thee a tale of truth,
Which I cond of Tityrus in my youth,
Keeping his sheepe on the hils of Kent?

CVDDIE.
To nought more, Thenot, my mind is bent,
Then to heare nouells of his deuise:
They bene so well thewed, and so wise,
What euer that good old man bespake.

THENOT.
Many meete tales of youth did he make,
And some of loue, and some of cheualrie:
But none fitter than this to applie.
Now listen a while, and hearken the end.
THere grewe an aged Tree on the greene,
A goodly Oake sometime had it bene,
With armes full strong and largely displayd,
But of their leaues they were disarayde:
The bodie bigge, and mightily pight,
Throughly rooted, and of wonderous hight:
Whilome had bene the King of the field,
And mochell mast to the husband did yielde,
And with his nuts larded many swine.
But now the gray mosse marred his rine,
His bared boughes were beaten with stormes,
His toppe was bald, & wasted with wormes,
His honor decayed, his braunches sere.
Hard by his side grew a bragging brere,
Which proudly thrust into Thelement,
And seemed to threat the Firmament.
Yt was embellisht with blossomes fayre,
And thereto aye wonned to repayre
The shepheards daughters, to gather flowres,
To peinct thir girlonds with his colowres.
And in his small bushes vsed to shrowde
The sweete Nightingale singing so lowde:
Which made this foolish Brere wexe so bold,
That on a time he cast him to scold,
And snebbe the good Oake, for he was old.
Why standst there (quoth he) thou brutish blocke?
Nor for fruict, nor for shadowe serues thy stocke:
Seest, how fresh my flowers bene spredde,
Dyed in Lilly white, and Cremsin redde,
With leaves engrained in lusty greene,
Colours meete to clothe a mayden Queene.
Thy wast bignes but combers the grownd,
And dirks the beauty of my blossomes rownd.
The mouldie mosse, which thee accloieth,
My Sinnamon smell too much annoieth.
Wherefore soone I rede thee, hence remove,
Least thou the price of my displeasure proue.
So spake this bold brere with great disdaine:
Little him answered the Oake againe,
But yielded, with shame and greefe adawed,
That of a weede he was ouerawed.
Yt chaunced after vpon a day,
The Hus-bandman selfe to come that way,
Of custome to seruewe his grownd,
And his trees of state in compasse rownd.
Him when the spitefull brere had espyed,

Causlesse complained, and lowdly cryed
Vnto his Lord, stirring vp sterne strife:
O my liege Lord, the God of my life,
Pleaseth you ponder your Suppliants plaint,
Caused of wrong, and cruell constraint,
Which I your poore Vassall dayly endure:
And but your goodnes the same recure,
Am like for desperate doole to dye,
Through felonous force of mine enemie.
Greatly aghast with this piteous plea,
Him rested the goodman on the lea,
And badde the Brere in his plaint proceede.
With painted words tho gan this proude weede,
(As most vsen Ambitious folke
His colowred crime with craft to cloke.
Ah my soueraigne, Lord of creatures all,
Thou placer of plants both humble and tall,
Was not I planted of thine owne hand,
To be the primrose of all thy land,
With flowring blossomes, to furnish the prime,
And scarlot berries in Sommer time?
How falls it then, that this faded Oake,
Whose bodie is sere, whose braunches broke,
Whose naked Armes stretch vnto the fyre,
Vnto such tyrannie doth aspire:
Hindering with his shade my louely light,
And robbing me of the swete sonnes sight?
So beate his old boughes my tender side,
That oft the bloud springeth from wounds wyde:
Vntimely my flowres forced to fall,
That bene the honor of your Coranall.
And oft he lets his cancker wormes light
Vpon my braunches, to worke me more spight:
And oft his hoarie locks downe doth cast,
Where with my fresh flowretts bene defast.
For this, and many more such outrage,
Crauing your goodlihead to aswage
The ranckorous rigour of his might,
Nought aske I, but onely to hold my right:
Submitting me to your good sufferance,
And praying to be garded from greeuance.
To this the Oake cast him to replie
Well as he couth: but his enemie
Had kindled such coles of displeasure,
That the good man noulde stay his leasure,
But home him hasted with furious heate,
Encreasing his wrath with many a threate.
His harmefull Hatchet he hent in hand,
(Alas, that it so ready should stand)
And to the field alone he speedeth.
(Ay little helpe to harme there needeth)
Anger nould let him speake to the tree,

Enaunter his rage mought cooled bee:
But to the roote bent his sturdy stroke,
And made many wounds in the wast Oake.
The Axes edge did oft turne againe,
As if halfe vnwilling to cutte the graine:
Semed, the sencelesse yron dyd feare,
Or to wrong holy eld did forbeare.
For it had bene an auncient tree,
Sacred with many a mysteree,
And often crost with the priestes crewe,
And often halowed with holy water dewe.
But sike fancies weren foolerie,
And broughten this Oake to this miserye.
For nought mought they quitten him from decay:
For fiercely the good man at him did laye.
The blocke oft groned vnder the blow,
And sighed to see his neare ouerthrow.
In fine the steele had pierced his pith,
Tho downe to the earth he fell forthwith:
His wonderous weight made the grounde to quake,
Thearth shronke vnder him, and seemed to shake.
There lyeth the Oake, pitied of none.
Now stands the Brere like a Lord alone,
Puffed vp with pryde and vaine pleasaunce:
But all this glee had no continuaunce.
For eftsones Winter gan to approche,
The blustring Boreas did encroche,
And beate vpon the solitarie Brere:
For nowe no succoure was seene him nere.
Now gan he repent his pryde to late:
For naked left and disconsolate,
The byting frost nipt his stalke dead,
The watrie wette weighed downe his head,
And heaped snowe burdned him so sore,
That nowe vpright he can stand no more:
And being downe, is trodde in the durt
Of cattell, and brouzed, and sorely hurt.
Such was thend of this Ambitious brere,
For scorning Eld

CVDDIE.
Now I pray thee shepheard, tel it not forth:
Here is a long tale, and little worth.
So longe haue I listned to thy speche,
That graffed to the ground is my breache:
My hartblood is welnigh frorne I feele,
And my galage growne fast to my heele:
But little ease of thy lewd tale I tasted.
Hye thee home shepheard, the day is nigh wasted.

Willye.
THomalin, why sytten we soe,
As weren ouerwent with woe,
Vpon so fayre a morow?
The ioyous time now nighest fast,
That shall alegge this bitter blast,
And slake the winters sorowe.

Thomalin.
Sicker Willye, thou warnest well:
For Winters wrath beginnes to quell,
And pleasant spring appeareth.
The grasse now ginnes to be refresht,
The Swallow peepes out of her nest,
And clowdie Welkin cleareth.

Willye.
Seest not thilke same Hawthorne studde,
How bragly it beginnes to budde,
And vtter his tender head?
Flora now calleth forth eche flower,
And bids make ready Maias bowre,
That newe is vpryst from bedde.
Tho shall we sporten in delight,
And learne with Lettice to wexe light,
That scornefully lookes askaunce,
Tho will we little Loue awake,
That nowe sleepeth in Lethe lake,
And pray him leaden our daunce.

Thomalin.
Willye, I wene thou bee assott:
For lustie Loue still sleepeth not,
But is abroad at his game.

Willye.
How kenst thou, that he is awoke?
Or hast thy selfe his slomber broke?
Or made preuie to the same?

Thomalin.
No, but happely I hym spyde,
Where in a bush he did him hide,
With winges of purple and blewe.
And were not, that my sheepe would stray,
The preuie marks I would bewray,
Whereby by chaunce I him knewe.

Willye.
Thomalin, haue no care for thy,
My selfe will haue a double eye,
Ylike to my flocke and thine:

For als at home I haue a syre,
A stepdame eke as whott as fyre,
That dewly adayes counts mine.

Thomalin.
Nay, but thy seeing will not serue,
My sheepe for that may chaunce to swerue,
And fall into some mischiefe.
For sithens is but the third morowe,
That I chaunst to fall a sleepe with sorowe,
And waked againe with griefe:
The while thilke same vnhappye Ewe,
Whose clouted legge her hurt doth shewe,
Fell headlong into a dell.
And there vnioynted both her bones:
Mought her necke bene ioynted attones,
She shoulde haue neede no more spell.
Thelf was so wanton and so wood,
(But now I trowe can better good)
She mought ne gang on the greene,

Willye.
Let be, as may be, that is past:
That is to come, let be forecast.
Now tell vs, what thou hast seene.

Thomalin.
It was vpon a holiday,
When shepheardes groomes han leaue to playe,
I cast to goe a shooting.
Long wandring vp and downe the land,
With bowe and bolts in either hand,
For birds in bushes tooting:
At length within an Yuie todde
(There shrouded was the little God)
I heard a busie bustling.
I bent my bow against the bush,
Listening if any thing did rushe,
But then heard no more rustling.
Tho peeping close into the thicke,
Might see the mouing of some quicke.
Whose shape appeared not:
But were it faerie, feend, or snake,
My courage earnd it to awake,
And manfully thereat shotte.
With that sprong forth a naked swayne,
With spotted winges like Peacocks trayne,
And laughing lope to a tree.
His gylden quiuer at his backe,
And silver bowe, which was but slacke,
Which lightly he bent at me.
That seeing, I leuelde againe,

And shott at him with might and maine,
As thicke, as it had hayled.
So long I shott, that al was spent:
Tho pumie stones I hastly hent,
And threwe: but nought availed:
He was so wimble, and so wight,
From bough to bough he lepped light,
And oft the pumies latched.
Therewith affrayd I ranne away:
But he, that earst seemd but to playe,
A shaft in earnest snatched,
And hit me running in the heele:
For then I little smart did feele:
But soone it sore encreased.
And now it ranckleth more and more,
And inwardly it festreth sore,
Ne wote I, how to cease it.

Willye.
Thomalin, I pittie thy plight.
Perdie with loue thou diddest fight:
I know him by a token.
For once I heard my father say,
How he him caught vpon a day,
(Whereof he wilbe wroken)
Entangled in a fowling net,
Which he for carrion Crowes had set,
That in our Peeretree haunted.
Tho sayd, he was a winged lad,
But bowe and shafts as then none had:
Els had he sore be daunted.
But see the Welkin thicks apace,
And stouping Phebus steepes his face:
Yts time to hast vs homeward.

Willyes Embleme.
To be wise and eke to loue,
Is graunted scarce to God aboue.

Thomalins Embleme.
Of Hony and of Gaule in loue there is store:
The Honye is much, but the Gaule is more.

The Shepheardes Calender: April
Tell me good Hobbinoll, what garres thee greete?
What? hath some Wolfe thy tender Lambes ytorne?
Or is thy Bagpype broke, that soundes so sweete?
Or art thou of thy loued lasse forlorne?

Or bene thine eyes attempred to the yeare,
Quenching the gasping furrowes thirst with rayne?

Like April shoure, so stremes the trickling teares
Adowne thy cheeke, to quenche thy thristye payne.

HOBBINOLL
Nor thys, nor that, so muche doeth make me mourne,
But for the ladde, whome long I lovd so deare,
Nowe loves a lasse, that all his love doth scorne:
He plongd in payne, his tressed locks dooth teare.

Shepheards delights he dooth them all forsweare,
Hys pleasaunt Pipe, whych made us meriment,
He wylfully hath broke, and doth forbeare
His wonted songs, wherein he all outwent.

THENOT
What is he for a Ladde, you so lament?
Ys love such pinching payne to them, that prove?
And hath he skill to make so excellent,
Yet hath so little skill to brydle love?

HOBBINOLL
Colin thou kenst, the Southerne shepheardes boye:
Him Love hath wounded with a deadly darte.
Whilome on him was all my care and joye,
Forcing with gyfts to winne his wanton heart.

But now from me hys madding mynd is starte,
And woes the Widdowes daughter of the glenne:
So nowe fayre Rosalind hath bredde hys smart,
So now his frend is chaunged for a frenne.

THENOT
But if hys ditties bene so trimly dight,
I pray thee Hobbinoll, recorde some one:
The whiles our flockes doe graze about in sight,
And we close shrowded in thys shade alone.

HOBBINOLL
Contented I: then will I singe his laye
Of fayre Elisa, Queene of shepheardes all:
Which once he made, as by a spring he laye,
And tuned it unto the Waters fall.

Ye dayntye Nymphs, that in this blessed Brooke
doe bathe your brest,
Forsake your watry bowres, and hether looke,
at my request:
And eke you Virgins, that on Parnasse dwell,
Whence floweth Helicon the learned well,
Helpe me to blaze
Her worthy praise,
Which in her sexe doth all excell.

Of fayre Eliza be your silver song,
that blessed wight:
The flowre of Virgins, may shee florish long,
In princely plight.
For shee is Syrinx daughter without spotte,
Which Pan the shepheards God of her begot:
So sprong her grace
Of heavenly race,
No mortall blemishe may her blotte.

See, where she sits upon the grassie greene,
(O seemely sight)
Yclad in Scarlot like a mayden Queene,
And Ermines white.
Upon her head a Cremosin coronet,
With Damaske roses and Daffadillies set:
Bayleaves betweene,
And Primroses greene
Embellish the sweete Violet.

Tell me, have ye seene her angelick face,
Like Ph{oe}be fayre?
Her heavenly haveour, her princely grace
can you well compare?
The Redde rose medled with the White yfere,
In either cheeke depeincten lively chere.
Her modest eye,
Her Majestie,
Where have you seene the like, but there?

I sawe Ph{oe}bus thrust out his golden hedde,
upon her to gaze:
But when he sawe, how broade her beames did spredde,
it did him amaze.
He blusht to see another Sunne belowe,
Ne durst againe his fyrye face out showe:
Let him, if he dare,
His brightnesse compare
With hers, to have the overthrowe.

Shewe thy selfe Cynthia with thy silver rayes,
and be not abasht:
When shee the beames of her beauty displayes,
O how art thou dasht?
But I will not match her with Latonaes seede,
Such follie great sorow to Niobe did breede.
Now she is a stone,
And makes dayly mone,
Warning all other to take heede.

Pan may be proud, that ever he begot

such a Bellibone,
And Syrinx rejoyse, that ever was her lot
to beare such an one.
Soone as my younglings cryen for the dam,
To her will I offer a milkwhite Lamb:
Shee is my goddesse plaine,
And I her shepherds swayne,
Albee forswonck and forswatt I am.

I see Calliope speede her to the place,
where my Goddesse shines:
And after her the other Muses trace,
with their Violines.
Bene they not Bay braunches, which they doe beare,
All for Elisa in her hand to weare?
So sweetely they play,
And sing all the way,
That it a heaven is to heare.

Lo how finely the graces can it foote
to the Instrument:
They dauncen deffly, and singen soote,
in their meriment.
Wants not a fourth grace, to make the daunce even?
Let that rowme to my Lady be yeven:
She shalbe a grace,
To fyll the fourth place,
And reigne with the rest in heaven.

And whither rennes this bevie of Ladies bright,
raunged in a rowe?
They bene all Ladyes of the lake behight,
that unto her goe.
Chloris, that is the chiefest Nymph of al,
Of Olive braunches beares a Coronall:
Olives bene for peace,
When wars doe surcease:
Such for a Princesse bene principall.

Ye shepheards daughters, that dwell on the greene,
hye you there apace:
Let none come there, but that Virgins bene,
to adorne her grace.
And when you come, whereas shee is in place,
See, that your rudeness doe not you disgrace:
Binde your fillets faste,
And gird in your waste,
For more finesse, with a tawdrie lace.

Bring hether the Pincke and purple Cullambine,
With Gelliflowres:
Bring Coronations, and Sops in wine,

worne of Paramoures.
Strowe me the ground with Daffadowndillies,
And Cowslips, and Kingcups, and loved Lillies:
The pretie Pawnce,
And the Chevisaunce,
Shall match with the fayre flowre Delice.

Now ryse up Elisa, decked as thou art,
in royall aray:
And now ye daintie Damsells may depart
echeone her way,
I feare, I have troubled your troupes to longe:
Let dame Eliza thanke you for her song.
And if you come hether,
When Damsines I gether,
I will part them all you among.

THENOT
And was thilk same song of Colins owne making?
Ah foolish boy, that is with love yblent:
Great pittie is, he be in such taking,
For naught caren, that bene so lewdly bent.

HOBBINOLL
Sicker I hold him, for a greater fon,
That loves the thing, he cannot purchase.
But let us homeward: for night draweth on,
And twincling starres the daylight hence chase.THENOTS EMBLEME

The Shepheardes Calender: May
PALINODE
Is not thilke the mery moneth of May,
When loue lads masken in fresh aray?
How falles it then, we no merrier bene,
Ylike as others, girt in gawdy greene?
Our blonket liueryes bene all to sadde,
For thilke same season, when all is ycladd
With pleasaunce: the grownd with grasse, the Wods
With greene leaues, the bushes with bloosming Buds.
Yougthes folke now flocken in euery where,
To gather may bus-kets and smelling brere:
And home they hasten the postes to dight,
And all the Kirke pillours eare day light,
With Hawthorne buds, and swete Eglantine,
And girlonds of roses and Sopps in wine.
Such merimake holy Saints doth queme,
But we here sytten as drownd in a dreme.

PIERS.
For Younkers Palinode such follies fitte,
But we tway bene men of elder witt.

PALINODE.
Sicker this morrowe, ne lenger agoe,
I sawe a shole of shepeheardes outgoe,
With singing, and shouting, and iolly chere:
Before them yode a lusty Tabrere,
That to the many a Horne pype playd,
Whereto they dauncen eche one with his mayd.
To see those folkes make such iouysaunce,
Made my heart after the pype to daunce.
Tho to the greene Wood they speeden hem all,
To fetchen home May with their musicall:
And home they bringen in a royall throne,
Crowned as king: and his Queene attone
Was Lady Flora, on whom did attend
A fayre flock of Faeries, and a fresh bend
Of louely Nymphes. (O that I were there,
To helpen the Ladyes their Maybush beare)
Ah Piers, bene not thy teeth on edge, to thinke
How great sport they gaynen with little swinck.

PIERS.
Perdie so farre am I from enuie,
That their fondnesse inly I pitie.
Those faytours little regarden their charge,
While they letting their sheepe runne at large,
Passen their time, that should be sparely spent,
In lustihede and wanton meryment.
Thilke same bene shepeheards for the Deuils stedde,
That playen while their flockes be vnfedde.
Well is it seene, theyr sheepe bene not their owne,
That letten them runne at randon alone.
But they bene hyred for little pay
Of other, that caren as little as they,
What fallen the flocke, so they han the fleece,
And get all the gayne, paying but a peece.
I muse, what account both these will make,
The one for the hire, which he doth take,
And thother for leauing his Lords tas-ke,
When [great] Pan account of shepeherdes shall aske.

PALINODE.
Sicker now I see thou speakest of spight,
All for thou lackest somedele their delight.
I (as I am) had rather be enuied,
All were it of my foe, then fonly pitied:
And yet if neede were, pitied would be,
Rather, then other should scorne at me:
For pittied is mishappe, that nas remedie,
But scorned bene dedes of [fond] foolerie.
What shoulden shepheards other things tend,
Then sith their God his good does them send,

Reapen the fruite thereof, that is pleasure,
The while they here liuen, at ease and leasure?
For when they bene dead, their good is ygoe,
They sleepen in rest, well as other moe.
Tho with them wends, what they spent in cost,
But what they left behind them, is lost.
Good is no good, but if it be spend:
God giueth good for none other end.

PIERS.
Ah Palinodie, thou art a worldes childe:
Who touches Pitch mought needes be defilde.
But shepheards (as Algrind vsed to say,)
Mought not liue ylike, as men of the laye:
With them it sits to care for their heire,
Enaunter their heritage doe impaire:
They must prouide for meanes of maintenaunce,
And to continue their wont countenaunce.
But shepheard must walke another way,
Sike worldly souenance he must foresay.
The sonne of his loines why should he regard
To leaue enriched with that he hath spard?
Should not thilke God, that gaue him that good,
Eke cherish his child, if in his wayes he stood?
For if he misliue in leudnes and lust,
Little bootes all the welth and the trust,
That his father left by inheritaunce:
All will be soone wasted with misgouernaunce.
But through this, and other their miscreaunce,
They maken many a wrong cheuisaunce,
Heaping vp waues of welth and woe,
The floddes whereof shall them ouerflowe.
Sike mens follie I cannot compare
Better, then to the Apes folish care,
That is so enamoured of her young one,
(And yet God wote, such cause hath she none)
That with her hard hold, and straight embracing,
She stoppeth the breath of her youngling.
So often times, when as good is meant,
Euil ensueth of wrong entent.
The time was once, and may againe retorne,
(For ought may happen, that hath bene beforne)
When shepeheards had none inheritaunce,
Ne of land, nor fee in sufferaunce:
But what might arise of the bare sheepe,
(Were it more or lesse) which they did keepe.
Well ywis was it with shepheards thoe:
Nought hauing, nought feared they to forgoe.
For Pan himselfe was their inheritaunce,
And little them serued for their mayntenaunce.
The [shepheards] God so wel them guided,
That of nought they were vnprouided,

Butter enough, honye, milke, and whay,
And their flockes fleeces, them to araye.
But tract of time, and long prosperitie:
That nource of vice, this of insolencie,
Lulled the shepheards in suc securitie,
That not content with loyal obeysaunce,
Some gan to gape for greedie gouernaunce,
And match them selfe with mighty potentates,
Louers of Lordship and troublers of states:
Tho gan shepheards swaines to looke a loft,
And leaue to liue hard, and learne to ligge soft:
Tho vnder colour of shepeheards, somewhile
There crept in Wolues, ful of fraude and guile,
That often deuoured their owne sheepe,
And often the shepheards, that did hem keepe.
This was the first sourse of shepheards sorowe,
That now nill be quitt with baile, nor borrowe.

PALINODE.
Three things to beare, bene very burdenous,
But the fourth to forbeare, is outragious.
Wemen that of Loues longing once lust,
Hardly forbearen, but haue it they must:
So when choler is inflamed with rage,
Wanting reuenge, is hard to asswage:
And who can counsell a thristie soule,
With patience to forbeare the offred bowle?
But of all burdens, that a man can beare,
Moste is, a fooles talke to beare and to heare.
I wene the Geaunt has not such a weight,
That beares on his shoulders the heauens height.
Thou findest faulte, where nys to be found,
And buildest strong warke vpon a weake ground:
Thou raylest on right withouten reason,
And blamest hem much, for small encheason.
How shoulden shepheardes liue, if not so?
What? should they pynen in payne and woe?
Nay sayd I thereto, by my deare borrowe,
If I may rest, I nill liue in sorrowe.
Sorrowe ne neede be hastened on:
For he will come without calling anone.
While times enduren of tranqullitie,
Vsen we freely our felicitie.
For when approchen the stormie stowres,
We mought with our shoulders beare of the sharpe showres.
And sooth to sayne, nought seemeth sike strife,
That shepheardes so witen ech others life,
And layen her faults the world beforne,
The while their foes done eache of hem scorne.
Let none mislike of that may not be mended:
So conteck soone by concord mought be ended.

PIERS.
Shepheard, I list none accordaunce make
With shepheard, that does the right way forsake.
And of the twaine, if choice were to me,
Had leuer my foe, then my freend he be.
For what concord han light and darke sam?
Or what peace has the Lion with the Lambe?
Such faitors, when their false harts bene hidde,
Will doe, as did the Foxe by the Kidde.

PALINODE.
Now Piers, of felowship, tell vs that saying:
For the Ladde can keepe both our flocks from straying.

PIERS.
THilke same Kidde (as I can well deuise
Was too very foolish and vnwise.
For on a tyme in Sommer season,
The Gate her dame, that had good reason,
Yode forth abroade vnto the greene wood,
To brouze, or play, or what shee thought good.
But for she had a motherly care
Of her young sonne, and wit to beware,
Shee set her youngling before her knee,
That was both fresh and louely to see,
And full of fauour, as kidde mought be:
His Vellet head began to shoot out,
And his wreathed hornes gan newly sprout:
The blossomes of lust to bud did beginne,
And spring forth ranckly vnder his chinne.
My sonne (quoth she) (and with that gan weepe:
For carefull thoughts in her heart did creepe)
God blesse thee poore Orphane, as he mought me,
And send thee ioy of thy iollitee.
Thy father (that word she spake with payne:
For a sigh had nigh rent her heart in twaine)
Thy father, had he liued this day,
To see the braunche of his body displaie,
How would he haue ioyed at this sweete sight?
But ah false Fortune such ioy did him spight,
And cutte of hys dayes with vntimely woe,
Betraying him into the traines of hys foe.
Now I a waylfull widdowe behight,
Of my old age haue this one delight,
To see thee succeede in thy fathers steade,
And florish in flowres of lusty head.
For euen so thy father his head vpheld,
And so his hauty hornes did he weld.
Tho marking him with melting eyes,
A thrilling throbbe from her hart did aryse,
And interrupted all her other speache,
With some old sorowe, that made a new breache:

Seemed shee sawe in the younglings face
The old lineaments of his fathers grace.
At last her solein silence she broke,
And gan his newe budded beard to stroke.
Kiddie (quoth shee) thou kenst the great care,
I have of thy health and thy welfare,
Which many wylde beastes liggen in waite,
For to entrap in thy tender state:
But most the Foxe, maister of collusion:
For he has voued thy last confusion.
For thy my Kiddie be ruld by mee,
And neuer giue trust to his trecheree.
And if he chaunce come, when I am abroade,
Sperre the yate fast for feare of fraude:
Ne for all his worst, nor for his best,
Open the dore at his request.
So schooled the Gate her wanton sonne,
That answerd his mother, all should be done.
Tho went the pensife Damme out of dore,
And chaunst to stomble at the threshold flore:
Her stombling steppe some what her amazed,
(For such, as signes of ill luck bene dispraised)
Yet forth shee yode thereat halfe aghast:
And Kiddie the dore sperred after her fast.
It was not long, after shee was gone,
But the false Foxe came to the dore anone:
Not as a Foxe, for then he had be kend,
But all as a poore pedlar he did wend,
Bearing a trusse of tryfles at hys backe,
As bells, and babes, and glasses in hys packe.
A Biggen he had got about his brayne,
For in his headpeace he felt a sore payne.
His hinder heele was wrapt in a clout,
For with great cold he had gotte the gout.
There at the dore he cast me downe hys pack,
And layd him downe, and groned, Alack, Alack.
Ah deare Lord, and sweet Saint Charitee,
That some good body woulde once pitie mee.
Well heard Kiddie al this sore constraint,
And lenged to know the cause of his complaint:
Tho creeping close behind the Wickets clinck,
Preuelie he peeped out through a chinck:
Yet not so preuelie, but the Foxe him spyed:
For deceitfull meaning is double eyed.
Ah good young maister (then gan he crye)
Iesus blesse that sweete face, I espye,
And keepe your corpse from the carefull stounds,
That in my carrion carcas abounds.
The Kidd pittying hys heauinesse,
Asked the cause of his great distresse,
And also who, and whence that he were.
Tho he, that had well ycond his lere,

Thus medled his talke with many a teare,
Sicke, sicke, alas, and little lack of dead,
But I be relieued by your beastlyhead.
I am a poore Sheepe, albe my coloure donne:
For with long traueile I am brent in the sonne.
And if that my Grandsire me sayd, be true,
Sicker I am very sybbe to you:
So be your goodlihead doe not disdayne
The base kinred of so simple swaine.
Of mercye and favour then I you pray,
With your ayd to forstall my neere decay.
Tho out of his packe a glasse he tooke:
Wherein while kiddie vnwares did looke,
He was so enamoured with the newell,
That nought he deemed deare for the iewell.
Tho opened he the dore, and in came
The false Foxe, as he were starke lame.
His tayle he clapt betwixt his legs twayne,
Lest he should be descried by his trayne.
Being within, the Kidde made him good glee,
All for the loue of the glasse he did see.
After his chere the Pedlar can chat,
And tell many lesings of this, and that:
And how he could shewe many a fine knack.
Tho shewed his ware, and opened his packe,
All saue a bell, which he left behind
In the bas-ket for the Kidde to fynd.
Which when the Kidde stooped down to catch,
He popt him in, and his bas-ket did latch,
Ne stayed he once, the dore to make fast,
But ran awaye with him in all hast.
Home when the doubtful Damme had her hyde,
She mought see the dore stand open wyde.
All aghast, lowdly she gan to call
Her Kidde: but he nould answere at all.
Tho on the flore she sawe the merchandise,
Of which her sonne had sette to dere a prise.
What helpe? her Kidde shee knewe well was gone:
Shee weeped, and wayled, and made great mone.
Such end had the Kidde, for he nould warned be
Of craft coloured with simplicitie:
And such end perdie does all hem remayne,
That of such false freendship bene fayne.

PALINODIE.
Truly Piers, thou art beside thy wit,
Furthest fro the marke, weening it to hit.
Now I pray thee, lette me thy tale borrowe
For our sir Iohn, to say to morrowe
At the Kerke, when it is holliday:
For well he meanes, but little can say.
But and if Foxes bene so crafty, as so,

Much needeth all shepheards hem to know.

PIERS.
Of their falshode more could I recount.
But now the bright Sunne gynneth to dismount:
And for the deawie night now doth nye,
I hold it best for vs, home to hye.

Palinodes Embleme.
[Pas men apiotos apistei]

Piers his Embleme.
[Tis d' ara piotis apisto]

The Shepheardes Calender: June
HOBBINOL.
LO! Collin, here the place, whose pleasaunt syte
From other shades hath weand my wandring mynde.
Tell me, what wants me here, to worke delyte?
The simple ayre, the gentle warbling wynde,
So calme, so coole, as no where else I fynde:
The grassye ground with daintye Daysies dight,
The Bramble bush, where Byrds of euery kynde
To the waters fall their tunes attemper right.

COLLIN.
O happy Hobbinoll, I blesse thy state,
That Paradise hast found, whych Adam lost.
Here wander may thy flock early or late,
Withouten dreade of Wolues to bene ytost:
Thy louely layes here mayet thou freely boste.
But I vnhappy man, whom cruell fate,
And angry Gods pursue from coste to coste,
Can nowhere fynd, to shouder my lucklesse pate.

HOBBINOLL.
Then if by me thou list aduised be,
Forsake the soyle, that so doth the bewitch:
Leaue me those hilles, where harbrough nis to see,
Nor holybush, nor brere, nor winding witche:
And to the dales resort, where shepheards ritch,
And fruictfull flocks bene euery where to see.
Here no night Rauens lodge more blacke then pitche,
Nor eluish ghosts, nor gastly owles doe flee.
But frendly Faeries, met with many Graces,
And lightfote Nymphes can chace the lingring night,
With Heydeguyes, and trimly trodden traces,
Whilst systers nyne, which dwell on Parnasse hight,
Doe make them musick, for their more delight:
And Pan himselfe to kisse their christall faces,
Will pype and daunce, when Phoebe shineth bright:

Such pierlesse pleasures haue we in these places.

COLLIN.
And I, whylst youth, and course of carelesse yeeres
Did let me walke withouten lincks of loue,
In such delights did ioy amongst my peeres:
But ryper age such pleasures doth reproue,
My fancye eke from former follies moue
To stayed steps: for time in passing weares
(As garments doen, which wexen old aboue)
And draweth newe delightes with hoary heares.
Tho couth I sing of loue, and tune my pype
Vnto my plaintiue pleas in verses made:
Tho would I seeke ,
To giue my Rosalind, and in Sommer shade
Dight gaudy Girlonds, was my comen trade,
To crowne her golden locks, but yeeres more rype,
And losse of her, whose loue as lyfe I wayd,
Those weary wanton toyes away dyd wype.

HOBBINOLL.
Colin, to heare thy rymes and roundelayes,
Which thou were wont on wastfull hylls to singe,
I more delight, then larke in Sommer dayes:
Whose Echo made the neyghbour groues to ring,
And taught the byrds, which in the lower spring
Did shroude in shady leaues from sonny rayes,
Frame to thy songe their chereful cheriping,
Or hold theyr peace, for shame of thy swete layes.
I sawe Calliope wyth Muses moe,
Soone as thy oaten pype began to sound,
Theyr youry Luyts and Tamburins forgoe:
And from the fountaine, where they sat around,
Renne after hastely thy siluer sound.
But when they came, where thou thy skill didst showe,
They drewe abacke, as halfe with shame confound,
Shepheard to see, them in theyr art outgoe.

COLLIN.
Of Muses Hobbinol, I conne no skill:
For they bene daughters of the hyghest Ioue,
And holden scorne of homely shepheards quill.
For sith I heard, that Pan with Phoebus stroue,
Which him to much rebuke and Daunger droue:
I neuer lyst presume to Parnasse hyll,
But pyping lowe in shade of lowly groue,
I play to please my selfe, all be it ill.
Nought weigh I, who my song doth prayse or blame,
Ne striue to winne renowne, or passe the rest:
With shepheard sittes not, followe flying fame:
But feede his flocke in fields, where falls hem best.
I wote my rymes bene rough, and rudely drest:

The fytter they, my carefull case to frame:
Enough is me to paint out my vnrest,
And poore my piteous plaints out in the same.

The God of shepheards Tityrus is dead,
Who taught me homely, as I can, to make.
He, whilst he liued, was the soueraigne head
Of shepheards all, that bene with loue ytake:
Well couth he wayle hys Woes, and lightly slake
The flames, which loue within his heart had bredd,
And tell vs mery tales, to keepe vs wake,
The while our sheepe about vs safely fedde.

Nowe dead he is, and lyeth wrapt in lead,
(O why should death on hym such outrage showe?)
And all hys passing skil with him is fledde,
The fame whereof doth dayly greater growe.
But if on me some little drops would flowe,
Of that the spring was in his learned hedde,
I soone would learne these woods, to wayle my woe,
And teache the trees, their trickling teares to shedde.

Then should my plaints, causd of discurtesee,
As messengers of all my painful plight,
Flye to my loue, where euer that she bee,
And pierce her heart with poynt of worthy wight:
As shee deserues, that wrought so deadly spight.
And thou Menalcas, that by trecheree
Didst vnderfong my lasse, to wexe so light,
Shouldest well be knowne for such thy villanee.

But since I am not, as I wish I were,
Ye gentle shepheards, which your flocks do feede,
Whether on hylls, or dales, or other where,
Beare witnesse all of thys so wicked deede:
And tell the lasse, whose flowre is woxe a weede,
And faultlesse fayth, is turned to faithlesse fere,
That she the truest shepheards hart made bleede,
That lyues on earth, and loued her most dere.

HOBBINOL.
O carefull Colin, I lament thy case,
Thy teares would make the hardest flint to flowe.
Ah faithlesse Rosalind, and voide of grace,
That art the roote of all this ruthfull woe.
But now is time, I gesse, homeward to goe:
Then ryse ye blessed flocks, and home apace,
Least night with stealing steppes doe you forsloe,
And wett your tender Lambes, that by you trace.

Colins embleme.
Gia speme spenta.

The Shepheardes Calender: July

Thomalin.
IS not thilke same a goteheard prowde,
that sittes on yonder bancke,
Whose straying heard them selfe doth shrowde
emong the bushes rancke?

Morrell.
What ho, thou iollye shepheards swayne,
come vp the hill to me:
Better is, then the lowly playne,
als for thy flocke, and thee.

Thomalin.
Ah God shield, man, that I should clime,
and learne to looke alofte,
This reede is ryfe, that oftentime
great clymbers fall vnsoft.
In humble dales is footing fast,
the trode is not so tickle:
And though one fall through heedlesse hast,
yet is his misse not mickle.
And now the Sonne hath reared vp
his fyriefooted teme,
Making his way betweene the Cuppe,
and golden Diademe:
The rampant Lyon hunts he fast,
with Dogge of noysome breath,
Whose balefull barking bringes in hast
pyne, plagues, and dreery death.
Agaynst his cruell scortching heate
where hast thou couerture?
The wastefull hylls vnto his threate
is a playne ouerture.
But if thee lust, to holden chat
with seely shepherds swayne,
Come downe, and learne the little what,
that Thomalin can sayne.

Morrell.
Syker, thous but a laesie loord,
and rekes much of thy swinck,
That with fond termes, and weetlesse words
to blere myne eyes doest thinke.
In euill houre thou hentest in hond
thus holy hylles to blame,
For sacred vnto saints they stond,
and of them han theyr name.
S. Michels mount who does not know,
that wardes the Westerne coste?

And of S. Brigets bowre I trow,
all Kent can rightly boaste:
And they that con of Muses skill,
sayne most what, that they dwell
(As goteheards wont) vpon a hill,
beside a learned well.
And wonned not the great god Pan,
vpon mount Oliuet:
Feeding the blessed flocke of Dan,
which dyd himselfe beget?

Thomalin.
O blessed sheepe, O shepheard great,
that bought his flocke so deare,
And them did saue with bloudy sweat
from Wolues, that would them teare.

Morrel.
Besyde, as holy fathers sayne,
there is a hyllye place,
Where Titan ryseth from the mayne,
to renne hys dayly race.
Vpon whose toppe the starres bene stayed,
and all the skie doth leane,
There is the caue, where Phebe layed,
The shepheard long to dreame.
Whilome there vsed shepheards all
to feede theyr flocks at will,
Till by his foly one did fall,
that all the rest did spill.
And sithens shepheardes bene foresayd
from places of delight:
For thy I weene thou be affrayed,
to clime this hilles height.
Of Synah can I tell thee more,
and of our Ladyes bowre:
But little needes to strow my store,
suffice this hill of our.
Here han the holy Faunes resourse,
and Syluanes haunten rathe.
Here has the salt Medway his sourse,
wherein the Nymphes doe bathe.
The salt Medway, that trickling stremis
adowne the dales of Kent:
Till with his elder brother Themis
his brackish waues be meynt.
Here growes Melampode euery where,
and Terebinth good for Gotes:
The one, my madding kiddes to smere,
the next, to heale theyr throtes.
Hereto, the hills bene nigher heuen,
and thence the passage ethe.

As well can proue the piercing levin,
that seeldome falls bynethe.

Thomalin.
Syker thou speakes lyke a lewde lorrell,
of Heauen to demen so:
How be I am but rude and borrell,
yet nearer wayes I knowe.
To Kerke the narre, from God more farre,
has bene an old sayd sawe.
And he that striues to touch the starres,
oft stombles at a strawe.
Alsoone may shepheard clymbe to skye,
that leades in lowly dales,
As Goteherd prowd that sitting hye,
vpon the Mountaine sayles.
My seely sheepe like well belowe,
they neede not Melampode:
For they bene hale enough, I trowe,
and liken theyr abode.
But if they with thy Gotes should yede,
they soone myght be corrupted:
Or like not of the frowie fede,
or with the weedes be glutted.
The hylls, where dwelled holy saints,
I reuerence and adore:
Not for themselfe, but for the sayncts,
which han be dead of yore.
And nowe they bene to heauen forewent,
theyr good is with them goe:
Theyr sample onely to vs lent,
that als we mought doe soe.
Shepheards they weren of the best,
and liued in lowly leas:
And sith theyr soules bene now at rest,
why done we them disease?
Such one he was, (as I haue heard
old Algrind often sayne)
That whilome was the first shepheard,
and liued with little gayne:
As meeke he was, as meeke mought be,
simple, as simple sheepe,
Humble, and like in eche degree
the flocke, which he did keepe.
Often he vsed of hys keepe
a sacrifice to bring,
Nowe with a Kidde, now with a sheepe
The Altars hallowing.
So lowted he vnto hys Lord,
such fauour couth he fynd,
That sithens neuer was abhord,
the simple shepheards kynd.

And such I weene the brethren were,
that came from Canaan:
The brethren twelue, that kept yfere
The flockes of mighty Pan.
But nothing such thilke shephearde was,
whom Ida hyll dyd beare,
That left hys flocke, to fetch a lasse,
whose loue he bought to deare:
For he was proude, that ill was payd,
(no such mought shepheards bee)
And with lewde lust was ouerlayd:
tway things doen ill agree:
But shepheard mought be meeke and mylde,
well eyed, as Argus was,
With fleshly follyes vndefyled,
and stoute as steede of brasse.
Sike one (sayd Algrin) Moses was,
that sawe hys makers face,
His face more cleare, then Christall glasse,
and spake to him in place.
This had a brother, (his name I knewe)
the first of all his cote,
A shepheard trewe, yet not so true,
as he that earst I hote.
Whilome all these were lowe, and lief,
and loued their flocks to feede,
They neuer strouen to be chiefe,
and simple was theyr weede.
But now (thanked be God therefore)
the world is well amend,
Their weedes bene not so nighly wore,
such simplesse mought them shend:
They bene yclad in purple and pall,
so hath theyr god them blist,
They reigne and rulen ouer all,
and lord it, as they list:
Ygyrt with belts of glitterand gold,
(mought they good sheepeheards bene)
Theyr Pan theyr sheepe to them has sold,
I saye as some haue seene.
For Palinode (if thou him ken)
yode late on Pilgrimage
To Rome, (if such be Rome) and then
he sawe thilke misusage.
For shepeheards (sayd he) there doen leade,
As Lordes done other where,
Theyr sheepe han crustes, and they the bread:
the chippes, and they the chere:
They han the fleece, and eke the flesh,
(O seely sheepe the while)
The corn is theyrs, let other thresh,
their hands they may not file.

They han great stores, and thriftye stockes,
great freendes and feeble foes:
What neede hem caren for their flocks?
theyr boyes can looke to those.
These wisardsweltre in welths waues,
pampred in pleasures deepe,
They han fatte kernes, and leany knaues,
their fasting flockes to keepe.
Sike mister men bene all misgone,
they heapen hylles of wrath:
Sike syrly shepheards han we none,
they keepen all the path.

Morell.
Here is a great deale of good matter,
lost for lacke of telling,
Now sicker I see, thou doest but clatter:
harme may come of melling.
Thou medlest more, then shall haue thanke,
to wyten shepheards welth:
When folke bene fat, and riches rancke,
it is a signe of helth.
But say to me, what is Algrin he,
that is so oft bynempt.

Thomalin.
He is a shepheard great in gree,
but hath bene long ypent.
One daye he sat vpon a hyll,
(as now thou wouldest me:
But I am tought by Algrins ill,
To loue the lowe degree.)
For sitting so with bared scalpe,
an Eagle sored hye,
That weening hys whyte head was chalke,
A shell fish downe let flye:
Shee weend the shell fish to haue broake,
but therewith bruzd his brayne,
So now astonied with the stroke,
he lyes in lingring payne.

Morrell.
Ah good Algrin, his hap was ill,
But shall be bett in time.
Now farwell shepheard, sith thys hyll
thou hast such doubt to climbe.

Thomalins Embleme.
In medio virtus.

Morrells Embleme.
In summo foelicitas

The Shepheardes Calender: August

Willye.
Ell me Perigot, what shalbe the game,
Wherefore with myne thou dare thy musick matche?
Or bene thy Bagpypes renne farre out of frame?
Or hath the Crampe thy ioynts benomd with ache?

Perigot.
Ah Willye, when the hart is ill assayde,
How can Bagpipe, or ioynts be well apayd?

Willye.
What the foule euill hath thee so bestadde?
Whilom thou was peregall to the best,
And wont to make the iolly shepeheards gladde
With pyping and dauncing, didst passe the rest.

Perigot.
Ah Willye now I haue learnd a newe daunce:
My old musick mard by a newe mischaunce.

Willye.
Mischiefe mought to that newe mischaunce befall,
That hath so raft vs of our meriment.
But reede me, what payne doth thee so appall?
Or louest thou, or bene thy younglings miswent?

Perigot.
Loue hath misled both my younglings, and mee:
I pyne for payne, and they my payne to see.

Willye.
Perdie and wellawaye: ill may they thriue:
Neuer knewe I louers sheepe in good plight.
But and if rymes with me thou dare striue,
Such fond fantsies shall soone be put to flight.

Perigot.
That shall I doe, though mochell worse I fared:
Neuer shall be sayde that Perigot was dared.

Willye.
Then loe Perigot the Pledge, which I plight:
A mazer ywrought of the Maple warre:
Wherein is enchased many a fayre sight
Of Beres and Tygres, that maken fiers warre:
And ouer them spred a goodly wild vine,
Entrailed with a wanton Yuie twine.
Thereby is a Lambe in the Wolues iawes:
But see, how fast renneth the shepheard swayne,

To saue the innocent from the beastes pawes:
And here with his shepehooke hath him slayne.
Tell me, such a cup hast thou euer sene?
Well mought it beseme any haruest Queene.

Perigot.
Thereto will I pawne yon spotted Lambe,
Of all my flocke there nis sike another:
For I brought him vp without the Dambe.
But Colin Clout rafte me of his brother,
That he purchast of me in the playne field:
Sore against my will was I forst to yield.

Willye.
Sicker make like account of his brother.
But who shall iudge the wager wonne or lost?

Perigot.
That shall yonder heardgrome, and none other,
Which ouer the pousse hetherward doth post.

Willye.
But for the Sunnebeame so sore doth vs beate,
Were not better, to shunne the scortching heate?

Perigot.
Well agreed Willy: then sitte thee downe swayne:
Sike a song neuer heardest thou, but Colin sing.

Cuddie.
Gynne, when ye lyst, ye iolly shepheards twayne:
Sike a iudge, as Cuddie, were for a king.

Perigot. T fell vpon a holly eue,

Willye. hey ho hollidaye,
Per. When holly fathers wont to shrieue:
Willye. now gynneth this roundelay.
Per. Sitting vpon a hill so hye,
Willye. hey ho the high hyll,
Per. The while my flocke did feede thereby,
Willye. the while the shepheard selfe did spill:
Per. I saw the bouncing Bellibone,
Willye. Hey ho Bonibell,
Per. Tripping ouer the dale alone,
Willye. she can trippe it very well:
Per. Well decked in a frocke of gray,
Willye. hey ho gray is greete,
Per. And in a Kirtle of greene saye,
Willye. the greene is for maydens meete:
Per. A chapelet on her head she wore,
Willye. hey ho chapelet,

Per. Of sweete Violets therein was store,
Willye. she sweeter than the Violet.
Per. My sheepe did leaue theyr wonted foode,
Willye. hey ho seely sheepe,
Per. And gazd on her, as they were wood,
Willye. woode as he, that did them keepe.
Per. As the bonilasse passed bye,
Willye. hey ho bonilasse,
Per. She roude at me with glauncing eye,
Willye. as cleare as the christall glasse:
Per. All as the Sunnye beame so bright,
Willye. hey ho the Sunne beame,
Per. Glaunceth from Phoebus face forthright,
Willye. so loue into thy hart did streame:
Per. Or as the thonder cleaues the cloudes,
Willye. hey ho the Thonder,
Per. Wherein the lightsome leuin shroudes,
Willye. so cleaues thy soule a sonder:
Per. Or as Dame Cynthias siluer raye
Willye. hey ho the Moonelight,
Per. Vpon the glittering waue doth playe:
Willye. such play is a pitteous plight.
Per. The glaunce into my heart did glide,
Willye. hey ho the glyder,
Per. Therewith my soule was sharply gryde,
Willye. uch wounds soone wexen wider.
Per. Hating to raunch the arrow out,
Willye. hey ho Perigot,
Per. I left the head in my hart roote:
Willye. it was a desperate shot.
Per. There it ranckleth ay more and more,
Willye. hey ho the arrowe,
Per. Ne can I find salue for my sore:
Willye. loue is a curelesse sorrowe.
Per. And though my bale with death I bought,
Willye. hey ho the heauie cheere,
Per. Yet should thilke lasse not from my thought:
Willye. so you may buye gold to deare.
Per. But whether in paynefull loue I pyne,
Willye. hey ho pinching payne,
Per. Or thriue in welth, she shalbe mine.
Willye. but if thou can her obteine.
Per. And if for gracelesse greefe I dye,
Willye. hey ho gracelesse griefe,
Per. Witnesse, shee slewe me with her eye:
Willye. let thy follye be the priefe.
Per. And you, that sawe it, simple shepe,
Willye. hey ho the fayre flocke,
Per. For priefe thereof, my death shall weepe,
Willye. and mone with many a mocke.
Per. So learnd I loue on a hollye eue,
Willye. hey ho hollidaye,

Per. That euer since my hart did greue.
Willye. now endeth our roundelay.

Cuddye.
Sicker sike a roundle neuer heard I none.
Little lacketh Perigot of the best.
And Willye is not greatly ouergone,
So weren his vndersongs well addrest.

Willye.
Herdgrome, I feare me, thou haue a squint eye:
Areede vprightly, who has the victorye?

Cuddie.
Fayth of my soule, I deeme ech haue gayned.
For thy let the Lambe be Willye his owne:
And for Perigot so well hath hym payned,
To him be the wroughten mazer alone.

Perigot.
Perigot is well pleased with the doome.
Ne can Willye wite the witelesse herdgroome.

Willye.
Never dempt more right of beautye I weene,
The shepheard of Ida, that iudged beauties Queene.

Cuddie.
But tell me shepheards, should it not yshend
Your roundels fresh, to heare a dolefull verse
Of Rosalend (who knowes not Rosalend?)
That Colin made, ylke can I you rehearse.

Perigot.
Now say it Cuddie, as thou art a ladde:
With mery thing its good to medle sadde.

Willy.
Fayth of my soule, thou shalt ycrouned be
In Colins stede, if thou this song areede:
For neuer thing on earth so pleaseth me,
As him to heare, or matter of his deede.

Cuddie.
Then listneth ech vnto my heauy laye,
And tune your pypes as ruthful, as ye may.
E wastefull woodes beare witnesse of my woe,
Wherein my plaints did oftentimes resound:
Ye carelesse byrds are priuie to my cryes,
Which in your songs were wont to make a part:
Thou pleasaunt spring hast luld me oft a sleepe,
Whose streames my trickling teares did ofte augment.

Resort of people doth my greefs augment,
The walled townes do worke my greater woe:
The forest wide is fitter to resound
The hollow Echo of my carefull cryes,
I hate the house, since thence my loue did part,
Whose waylefull want debarres myne eyes from sleepe.
Let stremes of teares supply the place of sleepe:
Let all that sweete is, voyd: and all that may augment
My doole, drawe neare. More meete to wayle my woe,
Bene the wild woddes my sorrowes to resound,
Then bedde, or bowre, both which I fill with cryes,
When I them see so waist, and fynd no part
Of pleasure past. Here will I dwell apart
In gastful groue therefore, till my last sleepe
Doe close mine eyes: so shall I not augment
With sight of such a chaunge my recklesse woe:
Helpe me, ye banefull byrds, whose shrieking sound
Ys signe of dreery death, my deadly cryes
Most ruthfully to tune. And as my cryes
(Which of my woe cannot bewray least part)
You heare all night, when nature craueth sleepe,
Increase, so let your yrksome yells augment.
Thus all the night in plaints, the daye in woe
I vowed haue to wayst, till safe and sound
She home returne, whose voyces siluer sound
To cheerefull songs can chaunge my cherelesse cryes.
Hence with the Nightingale will I take part,
That blessed byrd, that spends her time of sleepe
In songs and plaintiue pleas, the more taugment
The memory of hys misdeede, that bred her woe:
And you that feele no woe, | when as the sound
Of these my nightly cryes | ye heare apart,
Let breake your sounder sleepe | and pitie augment.

Perigot.
O Colin, Colin, the shepheards ioye,
How I admire ech turning of thy verse:
And Cuddie, fresh Cuddie, the liefest boye,
How dolefully his doole thou didst rehearse.

Cuddie.
Then blowe your pypes shepheards, til you be at home:
The night nigheth fast, yts time to be gone.

Perigot his Embleme.
Vincenti gloria victi.

Willyes Embleme.
Vinto non vitto.

Cuddies Embleme.
Felice chi puo.

Hobbinol.
Diggon Dauie, I bidde her god day:
Or Diggon her is, or I missaye.

Diggon.
Her was her, while it was daye light,
But nowe her is a most wretched wight.
For day, that was, is wightly past,
And now at earst the dirke night doth hast.

Hobbinoll.
Diggon areede, who has thee so dight?
Neuer I wist thee in so poor a plight.
Where is the fayre flocke, thou was wont to leade?
Or bene they chaffred? or at mischiefe dead?

Diggon.
Ah for loue of that, is to thee moste leefe,
Hobbinol, I pray thee gall not my old griefe:
Sike question ripeth vp cause of newe woe,
For one opened mote vnfolde many moe.

Hobbinoll.
Nay, but sorrow close shrouded in hart
I know, to kepe, is a burdenous smart.
Eche thing imparted is more eath to beare:
When the rayne is faln, the cloudes wexen cleare.
And nowe sithence I sawe thy head last,
Thrise three Moones bene fully spent and past:
Since when thou hast measured much grownd,
And wandred I wene about the world rounde,
So as thou can many thinges relate:
But tell me first of thy flocks astate.

Diggon.
My sheepe bene wasted, (wae is me therefore)
The iolly shepheard that was of yore,
Is nowe nor iolloye, nor shepehearde more.
In forrein costes, men sayd, was plentye:
And so there is, but all of miserye.
I dempt there much to haue eeked my store,
But such eeking hath made my hart sore.
In tho countryes, whereas I haue bene,
No being for those, that truely mene,
But for such, as of guile maken gayne,
No such countrye, as there to remaine.
They setten to sale their shops of shame,
And maken a Mart of theyr good name.
The shepheards there robben one another,

And layen baytes to beguile her brother.
Or they will buy his sheepe out of the cote,
Or they will caruen the shepheards throte.
The shepheards swayne you cannot wel ken,
But it be by his pryde, from other men:
They looken bigge as Bulls, that bene bate,
And bearen the cragge so stiffe and so state,
As cocke on his dunghill, crowing cranck.

Hobbinoll.
Diggon, I am so stiffe, and so stanck,
That vneth may I stand any more:
And nowe the Westerne wind bloweth sore,
That nowe is in his chiefe souereigntee,
Beating the withered leafe from the tree.
Sitte we downe here under the hill:
Tho may we talke, and tellen our fill,
And make a mocke at the blustring blast.
Now say on Diggon, what euer thou hast.

Diggon.
Hobbin, ah hobbin, I curse the stounde,
That euer I cast to haue lorne this grounde.
Wel-away the while I was so fonde,
To leaue the good, that I had in honde,
In hope of better, that was vncouth:
So lost the Dogge the flesh in his mouth.
My seely sheepe (ah seely sheepe)
That here by there I whilome vsed to keepe,
All were they lustye, as thou didst see,
Bene all sterued with pyne and penuree.
Hardly my selfe escaped thilke payne,
Driuen for neede to come home agayne.

Hobbinoll.
Ah fon, now by thy losse art taught,
That seeldome chaunge the better brought.
Content who liues with tryed state,
Neede feare no chaunge of frowning fate:
But who will seeke for vnknowne gayne,
Oft liues by losse, and leaues with payne.

Diggon.
I wote ne Hobbin how I was bewitcht
With vayne desyre, and hope to be enricht.
But sicker so it is, as the bright starre
Seemeth ay greater, when it is farre:
I thought the soyle would haue made me rich:
But nowe I wote, it is nothing sich.
For eyther the shepeheards bene ydle and still,
And ledde of theyr sheepe, what way they wyll:
Or they bene false, and full of couetise,

And casten to compasse many wrong emprise.
But the more bene fraught with fraud and spight,
Ne in good nor goodnes taken delight:
But kindle coales of conteck and yre,
Wherewith they sette all the world on fire:
Which when they thinken agayne to quench
With holy water, they doen hem all drench.
They saye they con to heauen the high way,
But by my soule I dare vndersaye,
Thye neuer sette foote in that same troade,
But balk the right way, and strayen abroad.
They boast they han the deuill at commaund:
But aske hem therefore, what they han paund.
Marrie that great Pan bought with deare borrow,
To quite it from the blacke bowre of sorrowe.
But they han sold thilk same long agoe:
For thy woulden drawe with hem many moe.
But let hem gange alone a Gods name:
As they han brewed, so let hem beare blame.

Hobbinoll.
Diggon, I praye the speake not so dirke.
Such myster saying me seemeth to mirke.

Diggon.
Then playnely to speake of shepheards most what,
Badde is the best (this english is flatt.)
Their ill hauiour garres men missay,
Both of their doctrine, and of their faye.
They sayne the world is much war then it wont,
All for her shepheards bene beastly and blont.
Other sayne, but how truely I note,
All for they holden shame of theyr cote.
Some sticke not to say, (whote cole on her tongue)
That sike mischeife graseth hem emong,
All for the casten too much of worlds care,
To deck her Dame, and enrich her heyre:
For such encheason, If you goe nye,
Fewe chymneis reeking you shall espye:
The fat Oxe, that wont ligge in the stal,
Is nowe fast stalled in her crumenall.
Thus chatten the people in theyr steads,
Ylike as a Monster of many heads.
But they that shooten neerest the pricke,
Sayne, other the fat from their beards doen lick.
For bigge Bulles of Basanbrace hem about,
That with theyr hornes butten the more stoute:
But the leane soules treaden vnder foote.
And to seeke redresse mought little boote:
For liker bene they to pluck away more,
Then ought of the gotten good to restore.
For they bene like foule wagmoires ouergrast,

That if thy galage once sticketh fast,
The more to wind it out thou doest swinck,
Thou mought ay deeper and deeper sinck.
Yet better leaue of with a little losse,
Then by much wrestling to leese the grosse.

Hobbinoll.
Nowe Diggon, I see thou speakest to plaine:
Better it were, a little to feyne,
And cleanly couer, that cannot be cured.
Such il, as is forced, mought nedes be endured.
But of sike pastoures howe done the flocks creepe?

Diggon.
Sike as the shepheards, sike bene her sheepe,
For they nill listen to the shepheards voyce,
But if he call hem at theyr good choyce,
They wander at wil, and stray at pleasure,
And to theyr foldes yeeld at their owne leasure.
But they had be better come at their cal:
for many han into mischiefe fall,
And bene of rauenous Wolues yrent,
All for they nould be buxome and bent.

Hobbinoll.
Fye on thee Diggon, and all thy foule leasing,
Well is knowne that sith the Saxon king,
Neuer was Woolfe seene many nor some,
Nor in all Kent, nor in Christendome:
But the fewer Woolues (the soth to sayne,)
The more bene the Foxes that here remaine.

Diggon.
Yes, but they gang in more secrete wise,
And with sheepes clothing doen hem disguise,
They walke not widely as they were wont
For feare of raungers, and the great hunt:
But priuely prolling too and froe,
Enaunter they mought be inly knowe.

Hobbinoll.
Or priue or pert yf any bene,
We han great Bandogs will tear their skinne.

Diggon.
Indeede thy ball is a bold bigge curre,
And could make a iolly hole in theyr furre.
But not good Dogges hem needeth to chace,
But heedy shepheards to discerne their face.
For all their craft is in their countenaunce,
They bene so graue and full of mayntenaunce.
But shall I tell thee what my selfe knowe,

Chaunced to Roffynn not long ygoe?

Hobbinoll.
Say it out Diggon, what euer it hight,
For not but well mought him betight.
He is so meeke, wise, and merciable,
And with his word his worke is conuenable.
Colin clout I wene be his selfe boye,
(Ah for Colin he whilome my ioye)
Shepheards sich, God mought vs many send,
That doen so carefully theyr flocks tend.

Diggon.
Thilk same shepheard mought I well marke:
He has a Dogge to byte or to bark,
Neuer had shepheard so nene a kurre,
That waketh, and if but a leafe sturre.
Whilome there wonned a wicked Wolfe,
That with many a Lambe had glutted his gulfe.
And euer at night wont to repayre
Vnto the flocke, when the Welkin shone faire,
Ycladde in clothing of seely sheepe,
When the good old man vsed to sleepe.
Tho at midnight he would barke and ball,
(For he had eft learned a curres call.)
As if a Woolfe were emong the sheepe.
With that the shpheard would breake his sleepe,
And send out Lowder (for so his dog hote)
To raunge the fields with wide oppen throte.
Tho when as Lowder was farre away,
This Woluish sheepe would catchen his pray,
A Lambe, or a Kidde, or a weanell wast:
With that to the wood would he speede him fast.
Long time he vsed this slippery pranck,
Ere Roffy could for his laboure him thanck.
At end the shepheard his practise spyed,
(For Roffy is wise, and as Argus eyed)
And when at euen he came to the flocke,
Fast in theyr folds he did them locke,
And tooke out the Woolfe in his counterfect cote,
And let out the sheepes bloud at his throte.

Hobbinoll.
Marry Diggon, what should him affraye,
To take his owne where euer it laye?
For had his wesand bene a little widder,
He would hue deuoured both hidder and shidder.

Diggon.
Mischiefe light on him, and Gods great curse,
Too good for him had bene a great deale worse:
For it was a perilous beast aboue all,

And eke had he cond the shepherds call.
And oft in the night came to the shepecote,
And called Lowder, with a hollow throte,
As if it the old man selfe had bene.
The dog his maisters voice did it weene,
Yet halfe in doubt, he opened the dore,
And ranne out, as he was wont of yore.
No sooner was out, but swifter then thought,
Fast by the hyde the Wolfe lowder caught:
And had not Roffy renne to the steuen,
Lowder had be slaine thilke same euen.

Hobbinoll.
God shield man, he should so ill haue thriue,
All for he did his deuoyr beliue.
If sike bene Wolues, as thou hast told,
How mought we Diggon, hem be-hold.

Diggon.
How, but with heede and watchfulnesse,
Forstallen hem of their wilinesse?
For thy with shepheard sittes not playe,
Or sleepe, as some doen, all the long day:
But euer liggen in watch and ward,
From soddein force theyr flocks for to gard.

Hobbinoll.
Ah Diggon, thilke same rule were too straight,
All the cold season to wach and waite.
We bene of flesh, men as other bee,
Why should we be bound to such miseree?
What euer thing lacketh chaungeable rest,
Mought needes decay, when it is at best.

Diggon.
Ah but Hobbinol, all this long tale,
Nought easeth the care, that doth me forhaile.
What shall I doe? what way shall I wend,
My piteous plight and losse to amend?
Ah, good Hobbinol, mought I thee praye,
Of ayde or counsell in my decaye.

Hobbinoll.
Now by my soule Diggon, I lament
The haplesse mischief, that has thee hent,
Nethelesse thou seest my lowly saile,
That froward fortune doth euer auaile.
But were Hobbinoll, as God mought please,
Diggon should soone find fauour and ease.
But if to my cotage thou wilt resort,
So as I can, I wil thee comfort:
There mayst thou ligge in a vetchy bed,

Till fayrer Fortune shewe forth her head.

Diggon.
Ah Hobbinol, God mought it thee requite.
Diggon on fewe such freends did euer lite.

Diggons Embleme.
Inopem me copia fecit.

The Shepheardes Calender: October
Cuddie, for shame hold up thy heavye head,
And let us cast with what delight to chace,
And weary thys long lingring Phoebus race.
Whilome thou wont the shepheards laddes to leade,
In rymes, in ridles, and in bydding base:
Now they in thee, and thou in sleepe art dead.

CUDDY
Piers, I have pyped erst so long with payne,
That all mine Oten reedes bene rent and wore:
And my poore Muse hath spent her spared store,
Yet little good hath got, and much lesse gayne,
Such pleasaunce makes the Grashopper so poore,
And ligge so layd, when Winter doth her straine.

The dapper ditties, that I wont devise,
To feede youthes fancie, and the flocking fry,
Delighten much: what I the bett for thy?
They han the pleasure, I a sclender prise.
I beate the bush, the byrds to them doe flye:
What good thereof to Cuddie can arise?

PIERS
Cuddie, the prayse is better, then the price,
The glory eke much greater then the gayne:
O what an honor is it, to restraine
The lust of lawlesse youth with good advice:
Or pricke them forth with pleasaunce of thy vaine,
Whereto thou list their trayned willes entice.

Soone as thou gynst to sette thy notes in frame,
O how the rurall routes to thee doe cleave:
Seemeth thou dost their soule of sence bereave,
All as the shepheard, that did fetch his dame
From Plutoes balefull bowre withouten leave:
His musicks might the hellish hound did tame.

CUDDIE
So praysen babes the Peacoks spotted traine,
And wondren at bright Argus blazing eye:
But who rewards him ere the more for thy?

Or feedes him once the fuller by a graine?
Sike prayse is smoke, that sheddeth in the skye,
Sike words bene wynd, and wasten soone in vayne.

PIERS
Abandon then the base and viler clowne,
Lyft up thy selfe out of the lowly dust:
And sing of bloody Mars, of wars, of giusts.
Turne thee to those, that weld the awful crowne,
To doubted Knights, whose woundlesse armour rusts,
And helmes unbruzed wexen dayly browne.

There may thy Muse display her fluttryng wing,
And stretch her selfe at large from East to West:
Whither thou list in fayre Elisa rest,
Or if thee please in bigger notes to sing,
Advaunce the worthy whome shee loveth best,
That first the white beare to the stake did bring.

And when the stubborne stroke of stronger stounds,
Has somewhat slackt the tenor of thy string:
Of love and lustihed tho mayst thou sing,
And carrol lowde, and leade the Myllers rownde,
All were Elisa one of thilke same ring.
So mought our Cuddies name to Heaven sownde.

CUDDYE
Indeed the Romish Tityrus, I heare,
Through his Mec{oe}nas left his Oaten reede,
Whereon he earst had taught his flocks to feede,
And laboured lands to yield the timely eare,
And eft did sing of warres and deadly drede,
So as the Heavens did quake his verse to here.

But ah Mec{oe}nas is yclad in claye,
And great Augustus long ygoe is dead:
And all the worthies liggen wrapt in leade,
That matter made for Poets on to play:
For ever, who in derring doe were dreade,
The loftie verse of hem was loved aye.

But after vertue gan for age to stoupe,
And mighty manhode brought a bedde of ease:
The vaunting Poets found nought worth a pease,
To put in preace among the learned troupe.
Tho gan the streames of flowing wittes to cease,
And sonnebright honour pend in shamefull coupe.

And if that any buddes of Poesie,
Yet of the old stocke gan to shoote agayne:
Or it mens follies mote be forst to fayne,
And rolle with rest in rymes of rybaudrye:

Or as it sprong, it wither must agayne:
Tom Piper makes us better melodie.

PIERS
O pierlesse Poesye, where is then thy place?
If nor in Princes pallace thou doe sitt:
(And yet is Princes pallace the most fitt)
Ne brest of baser birth doth thee embrace.
Then make thee winges of thine aspyring wit,
And, whence thou camst, flye backe to heaven apace.

CUDDIE
Ah Percy it is all to weake and wanne,
So high to sore, and make so large a flight:
Her peeced pyneons bene not so in plight,
For Colin fittes such famous flight to scanne:
He, were he not with love so ill bedight,
Would mount as high, and sing as soote as Swanne.

PIERS
Ah fon, for love does teach him climbe so hie,
And lyftes him up out of the loathsome myre:
Such immortall mirrhor, as he doth admire,
Would rayse ones mynd above the starry skie.
And cause a caytive corage to aspire,
For lofty love doth loath a lowly eye.

CUDDIE
All otherwise the state of Poet stands,
For lordly love is such a Tyranne fell:
That where he rules, all power he doth expell.
The vaunted verse a vacant head demaundes,
Ne wont with crabbed care the Muses dwell.
Unwisely weaves, that takes two webbes in hand.

Who ever casts to compasse weightye prise,
And thinks to throwe out thondring words of threate:
Let powre in lavish cups and thriftie bitts of meate,
For Bacchus fruite is frend to Phoebus wise.
And when with Wine the braine begins to sweate,
The nombers flowe as fast as spring doth ryse.

Thou kenst not Percie howe the ryme should rage.
O if my temples were distaind with wine,
And girt in girlonds of wild Yvie twine,
How I could reare the Muse on stately stage,
And teache her tread aloft in buskin fine,
With queint Bellona in her equipage.

But ah my corage cooles ere it be warme,
For thy, content us in thys humble shade:
Where no such troublous tydes han us assayde,

Here we our slender pipes may safely charme.

PIERS
And when my Gates shall han their bellies layd:
Cuddie shall have a Kidde to store his farme.CUDDIES EMBLEME

Agitante calescimus illo
|&c|.

Thenot.
Colin my deare, when shall it please thee sing,
As thou were | wont songs of some iouisaunce?
Thy Muse to long slombreth in sorrowing,
Lulled a sleepe through loues misgouernaunce.
Now somewhat sing, whose endles souenaunce,
Emong the shepeheards swaines may aye remaine,
Whether thee list the loued lasse aduaunce,
Or honor Pan with hymnes of higher vaine.

Colin.
Thenot, now nis the time of merimake.
Nor Pan to herye, nor with loue to playe:
Sike myrth in May is meetest for to make,
Or summer shade vnder the cocked haye.
But nowe sadde Winter welked hath the day,
And Phoebus weary of his yerely tas-ke,
Ystabled hath his steedes in lowlye laye,
And taken vp his ynne in Fishes has-ke.
Thilke sollein season sadder plight doth aske:
And loatheth sike delightes, as thou doest prayse:
The mornefull Muse in myrth now list ne mas-ke,
As shee was wont in yougth and sommer dayes.
But if thou algate lust light virelayes,
And looser songs of loue to vnderfong
Who but thy selfe deserues sike Poetes prayse?
Relieue thy Oaten pypes, that sleepen long.

Thenot.
The Nightingale is souereigne of song,
Before him sits the Titmose silent bee:
And I vnfitte to thrust in [s]kilfull thronge,
Should Colin make iudge of my fooleree.
Nay, better learne of hem, that learned bee,
An han be watered at the Muses well:
The kindlye dewe drops from the higher tree,
And wets the little plants that lowly dwell.
But if sadde winters wrathe and season chill,
Accorde not with thy Muses meriment:
To sadder times thou mayst attune thy quill,
And sing of sorrowe and deathes dreeriment.

For deade is Dido, dead alas and drent,
Dido the greate shepehearde his daughter sheene:
The fayrest May she was that euer went,
Her like shee has not left behind I weene.
And if thou wilt bewayle my wofull tene:
I shall thee giue yond Cosset for thy payne:
And if thy rymes as rownd and rufull bene,
As those that did thy Rosalind complayne,
Much greater gyfts for guerdon thou shalt gayne,
Then Kidde of Cosset, which I thee bynempt:
Then vp I say, thou iolly shepeheard swayne,
Let not my small demaund be so contempt.

Colin.
Thenot to that I choose, thou doest me tempt,
But ah to well I wote my humble vaine,
And howe my rymes bene rugged and vnkempt:
Yet as I conne, my conning I will strayne.
Vp then Melpomene thou mounefulst Muse of nyne,
Such cause of mourning neuer hadst afore:
Vp grieslie ghostes and vp my rufull ryme,
Matter of myrth now shalt thou haue no more.
For dead she is, that myrth thee made of yore.
Didomy deare alas is dead,
Dead and lyeth wrapt in lead:
O heauie herse,
Let streaming teares be poured out in store:
O carefull verse.

Shepheards, that by your flocks on Kentish downes abyde,
Waile ye this wofull waste of natures warke:
Waile we the wight, whose presence was our pryde:
Waile we the wight, whose absence is our carke.
The sonne of all the world is dimme and darke:
The earth now lacks her wonted light,
And all we dwell in deadly night,
O heauie herse,
Breake we our pypes, that shrild as lowde as Larke,
O carefull verse.

Why do we longer liue, (ah why liue we so long)
Whose better dayes death hath shut vp in woe?
The fayrest floure our gyrlond all emong,
Is faded quite and into dust ygoe.
Sing now ye shepheards daughters, sing no moe
The songs that Colin made in her prayse,
But into weeping turne your wanton layes,
O heauie herse,
Now is time to dye. Nay time was long ygoe,
O carefull verse.

Whence is it, that the flouret of the field doth fade,

And lyeth buryed long in Winters bale:
Yet soone as spring his mantle hath displayd,
It floureth fresh, as it should neuer fayle?
But thing on earth that is of most auaile,
As vertues braunch and beauties budde,
Reliuen not for any good.
O heauie herse,
The braunch once dead, the budde eke needes must quaile,
O carefull verse.

She while she was, (that was, a woful word to sayne)
For beauties prayse and pleasaunce had no pere:
So well she couth the shepherds entertayne,
With cakes and cracknells and such country chere.
Ne would she scorne the simple shepheards swaine,
For she would call hem often heame
And giue hem curds and clouted Creame.
O heauie herse,
Als Colin cloute she would not once disdayne.
O carefull verse.

But nowe sike happy cheere is turnd to heauie chaunce,
Such pleasaunce now displast by dolors dint:
All Musick sleepes, where death doth leade the daunce,
And shepherds wonted solace is extinct.
The blew in black, the greene in gray is tinct,
The gaudie girlonds deck her graue,
The faded flowres her corse embraue.
O heauie herse,
Morne nowe my Muse, now morne with teares besprint.
O carefull verse.

O thou great shepheard Lobbin, how great is thy griefe,
Where bene the nosegayes that she dight for thee:
The coloured chaplets wrought with a chiefe,
The knotted rushrings, and gilte Rosemaree?
For shee deemed nothing too deere for thee.
Ah they bene all yclad in clay,
One bitter blast blew all away.
O heauie herse,
Thereof nought remaynes but the memoree.
O carefull verse.

Ay me that dreerie death should strike so mortall stroke,
That can vndoe Dame natures kindly course:
The faded lockes fall from the loftie oke,
The flouds do gaspe, for dryed is thyr sourse,
And flouds of teares flowe in theyr stead perforse.
The mantled medowes mourne,
Theyr sondry colours tourne.
O heauie herse,
The heauens doe melt in teares without remorse.

O carefull verse.

The feeble flocks in field refuse their former foode,
And hang theyr heads, as they would learne to weepe:
The beastes in forest wayle as they were woode,
Except the Wolues, that chase the wandring sheepe:
Now she is gon that safely did hem keepe.
The Turtle on the bared braunch,
Laments the wound, that death did launch.
O heauie herse,
And Philomele her song with teares doth steepe.
O carefull verse.

The water Nymphs, that wont with her to sing and daunce,
And for her girlond Oliue braunches beare,
Now balefull boughes of Cypres doen advaunce:
The Muses, that were wont greene bayes to weare,
Now bringen bitter Eldre braunches seare:
The fatall sisters eke repent,
Her vitall threde so soone was spent.
O heauie herse,
Mourne now my Muse, now mourne with heauie cheare.
O carefull verse.

O trustlesse state of earthly things, and slipper hope
Of mortal men, that swincke and sweate for nought,
And shooting wide, doe misse the marked scope:
Now haue I learnd (a lesson derely bought)
That nys on earth assuraunce to be sought:
For what might be in earthlie mould,
That did her buried body hould,
O heauie herse,
Yet saw I on the beare when it was brought,
O carefull verse.

But maugre death, and dreaded sisters deadly spight,
And gates of hel, and fyrie furies forse:
She hath the bonds broke of eternall night,
Her soule vnbodied of the burdenous corpse.
Why then weepes Lobbin so without remorse?
O Lobb, thy losse no longer lament,
Didonis dead, but into heauen hent.
O happye herse,
Cease now my Muse, now cease thy sorrowes sourse,
O ioyfull verse.

Why wayle we then? why weary we the Gods with playnts,
As if some euill were to her betight?
She raignes a goddesse now emong the saintes,
That whilome was the saynt of shepheards light:
And is enstalled nowe in heauens hight.
I see thee blessed soule, I see,

Walke in Elisian fieldes so free.
O happy herse,
Might I once come to thee (O that I might)
O ioyfull verse.

Vnwise and wretched men to weete whats good or ill,
We deeme of Death as doome of ill desert:
But knewe we fooles, what it vs bringes vntil,
Dye would we dayly, once it to expert.
No daunger there the shepheard can astert:
Fayre fieldes and pleasaunt layes there bene,
The fieldes ay fresh, the grasse ay greene:
O happy herse,
Make hast ye shepheards, thether to reuert,
O ioyfull verse.

Dido is gone afore (whose turne shall be the next?)
There liues shee with the blessed Gods in blisse,
There drincks she Nectar with Ambrosia mixt,
And ioyes enioyes, that mortall men do misse.
The honor now of highest gods she is,
That whilome was poore shepheards pryde,
While here on earth she did abyde.
O happy herse,
Ceasse now my song, my woe now wasted is.
O ioyfull verse.

Thenot.
Ay francke shepheard, how bene thy verses meint
With doolful pleasaunce, so as I ne wote,
Whether reioyce or weepe for great constrainte?
Thyne be the cossette, well hast thow it gotte.
Vp Colin vp, ynough thou mourned hast,
Noy gynnes to mizzle, hye we homeward fast.

Colins Embleme.
La mort ny mord.

The Shepheardes Calender: December
He gentle shepheard satte beside a springe,
All in the shadowe of a bushy brere,
That Colin hight, which wel could pype and singe,
For he of Tityrus his songs did lere.
There as he satte in secreate shade alone,
Thus gan he make of loue his piteous mone.
O soueraigne Pan thou God of shepheards all,
Which of our tender Lambkins takest keepe:
And when our flocks into mischaunce mought fall,
Doest save from mischeife the vnwary sheepe:
Als of their maisters hast no lesse regarde,
Then of the flocks, which thou doest watch and ward:

I thee beseche (so be thou deigne to heare,
Rude ditties tund to shepheards Oaten reede,
Or if I euer sonet song so cleare,
As it with pleasaunce mought thy fancie feede)
Hearken awhile from thy greene cabinet,
The rurall song of carefull Colinet.

Whilome in youth, when flowrd my ioyfull spring,
Like Swallow swift I wandred here and there:
For heate of heedlesse lust me so did sting,
That I of doubted daunger had no feare.
I went the wastefull woodes and forest wyde,
Withouten dreade of Wolues to bene espyed.

I wont to raunge amydde the mazie thickette,
And gather nuttes to make me Christmas game:
And ioyed oft to chace the trembling Pricket,
Or hunt the hartlesse hare, til shee were tame.
What wreaked I of wintrye ages waste,
Tho deemed I, my spring would euer laste.

How often haue I scaled the craggie Oke,
All to dislodge the Rauen of her neste:
Howe haue I wearied with many a stroke,
The stately Walnut tree, the while the rest
Vnder the tree fell all for nuts at strife:
For ylike to me was libertee and lyfe.

And for I was in thilke same looser yeares,
(Whether the Muse so wrought me from my birth,
Or I tomuch beleeued my shepherd peres)
Somedele ybent to song and musicks mirth,
A good olde shepheard, Wrenock was his name,
Made me by arte more cunning in the same.

Fro thence I durst in derring [doe] compare
With shepheards swayne, what euer fedde in field:
And if that Hobbinol right iudgement bare,
To Pan his owne selfe pype I neede not yield.
For if the flocking Nymphes did folow Pan,
The wiser Muses after Colin ranne.

But ah such pryde at length was ill repayde,
The shepheards God (perdie God was he none)
My hurtlesse pleasaunce did me ill vpbraide,
My freedome lorne, my life he lefte to mone.
Loue they him called, that gaue me checkmate,
But better mought they haue behote him Hate.

Tho gan my louely Spring bid me farewel,
And Sommer season sped him to display

(For loue then in the Lyons house did dwell)
The raging fyre, that kindled at his ray.
A comett stird vp that vnkindly heate,
That reigned (as men sayd) in Venus seate.

Forth was I ledde, not as I wont afore,
When choise I had to choose my wandring waye:
But whether luck and loues vnbridled lore
Would leade me forth on Fancies bitte to playe:
The bush my bedde, the bramble was my bowre,
The Woodes can witnesse many a wofull stowre.

Where I was wont to seeke the honey Bee,
Working her formall rowmes in Wexen frame:
The grieslie Todestool growne there mought I se
And loathed Paddocks lording on the same.
And where the chaunting birds luld me a sleepe,
The ghastlie Owle her grieuous ynne doth keepe.

Then as the springe giues place to elder time,
And bringeth forth the fruite of sommers pryde:
Also my age now passed yougthly pryme,
To thinges of ryper reason selfe applyed.
And learnd of lighter timber cotes to frame,
Such as might saue my sheepe and me fro shame.

To make fine cages for the Nightingale,
And Baskets of bulrushes was my wont:
Who to entrappe the fish in winding sale
Was better seene, or hurtful beastes to hont?
I learned als the signes of heauen to ken,
How Phoebe sayles, where Venus sittes and when.

And tryed time yet taught me greater thinges,
The sodain rysing of the raging seas:
The soothe of byrds by beating of their wings,
The power of herbs, both which can hurt and ease:
And which be wont tenrage the restlesse sheepe,
And which be wont to worke eternall sleepe.

But ah vnwise and witlesse Colin cloute,
That kydst the hidden kinds of many a wede:
Yet kydst not ene to cure thy sore hart roote,
Whose ranckling wound as yet does rifely bleede.
Why liuest thou stil, and yet hast thy deathes wound?
Why dyest thou stil, and yet aliue art founde?

Thus is my sommer worne away and wasted,
Thus is my haruest hastened all to rathe:
The eare that budded faire, is burnt & blasted,
And all my hoped gaine is turned to scathe.
Of all the seede, that in my youth was sowne,

Was nought but brakes and brambles to be mowne.

My boughes with bloosmes that crowned were at firste,
And promised of timely fruite such store,
Are left both bare and barrein now at erst:
The flattring fruite is fallen to grownd before.
And rotted, ere they were halfe mellow ripe:
My haruest wast, my hope away dyd wipe.

The fragrant flowres, that in my garden grewe,
Bene withered, as they had bene gathered long.
Theyr rootes bene dryed vp for lacke of dewe,
Yet dewed with teares they han be euer among.
Ah who has wrought my Ro[s]alind this spight
To spil the flowres, that should her girlond dight,

And I, that whilome wont to frame my pype,
Vnto the shifting of the shepheards foote:
Sike follies nowe haue gathered as too ripe,
And cast hem out, as rotten an vnsoote.
The loser Lasse I cast to please nomore,
One if I please, enough is me therefore.

And thus of all my haruest hope I haue
Nought reaped but a weedye crop of care:
Which, when I thought haue thresht in swelling sheaue,
Cockel for corne, and chaffe for barley bare.
Soone as the chaffe should in the fan be fynd,
All was blowne away of the wauering wynd.

So now my yeare drawes to his latter terme,
My spring is spent, my sommer burnt vp quite:
My harueste hasts to stirre vp winter sterne,
And bids him clayme with rigorous rage hys right.
So nowe he stormes with many a sturdy stoure,
So now his blustring blast eche coste doth scoure.

The carefull cold hath nypt my rugged rynde,
And in my face deepe furrowes eld hath pight:
My head besprent with hoary frost I fynd,
And by myne eie the Crow his clawe dooth wright.
Delight is layd abedde, and pleasure past,
No sonne now shines, cloudes han all ouercast.

Now leaue ye shepheards boyes yo[u]r merry glee,
My Muse is hoarse and weary of thys stounde:
Here will I hang my pype vpon this tree,
Was neuer pype of reede did better sounde.
Winter is come, that blowes the bitter blaste,
And after Winter dreerie death does hast.

Gather ye together my little flocke,

My little flock, that was to me so liefe:
Let me, ah lette me in your folds ye lock,
Ere the breme Winter breede you greater griefe.
Winter is come, that blowes the balefull breath,
And after Winter commeth timely death.

Adieu delightes, that lulled me asleepe,
Adieu my deare, whose loue I bought so deare:
Adieu my little Lambes and loued sheepe,
Adieu ye Woodes that oft my witnesse were:
Adieu good Hobbinol, that was so true,
Tell Rosalind, her Colin bids her adieu.

Colins Embleme.
[Vivitur ingenio, caetera mortis erunt.]

www.ingramcontent.com/pod-product-compliance
Lightning Source LLC
Chambersburg PA
CBHW060056050426
42448CB00011B/2481